Scripture Relief

Anxiety and Fear

Andrew O'Donnell

Copyright © 2011 by Andrew O'Donnell

All rights reserved. No part of this book may be reproduced, scanned, or distributed in any printed or electronic form without permission. Please do not participate in or encourage piracy of copyrighted materials in violation of the author's rights. Purchase only authorized editions.

Special thanks to Sarah Catherine O'Donnell, Elizabeth O'Donnell, and Julie McDermott

To the reader

2:18 a.m.

August 25th

2005

I woke up in a pool of sweat. My single bedroom apartment was still. There was no noise, no light, just darkness. My heart pounded in my chest even though I had just *woken up from a deep sleep. Experiencing chest pain, and unable to control my heartbeat, I sat on my bathroom floor in hopes of calming myself and stopping the sweat with the feel of the cool tile on my legs. I sat there for the next two hours. Silent. Shaking. Alone. I was not physically ill, nor was I having a heart attack; I was having a panic attack. This was one of many that I would endure, almost daily, for the next five years. I was a slave to my anxiety. There was no warning. At the time, I had no solution. Inexplicable fear and anxiety in my heart overwhelmed my entire being.*

    The biblical passages in this book are what helped me conquer my overwhelming stress, fear, and anxiety. The selections in this book are designed to serve as a resource and a guide of what the bible says about these topics. Often I would turn to the Bible, but not know where to start; or even where to look. Not knowing what I was looking for, I would open my Bible blindly and then, using what I like to call "pointing and praying," I would hope that the passage my finger landed on would be the answer to my troubles.

For those who are lucky enough to have a support system in place, whether it friends, family, community, it may be normal to be guided toward a certain passage that may have worked for others in times of trouble. Unfortunately for many that is where the guidance stops. Whether a seasoned reader of the Bible, or someone who has little to no exposure to the Bible, it is the goal of this book to act as a guide for those who are in need. Of course to gain a thorough understanding of these passages and their meanings, the best course of action is to submerse oneself in scripture. It is in the Word that one can find solace.

With a first hand understanding that in times of fear, stress, and anxiety the following passages can help the reader; it is not uncommon to ask the questions as to "who wrote this? What were the events surrounding the passage? Why it was written? Although uplifting, who were the players, and how does their story correlate with mine? What does this all mean for me?" The passages in this book fill in the gaps. This book is designed to act as a guide to what I found healing in the Old and New Testament. These words are not the words of a psychologist; or aimed to act as counsel in dealing with personal grief. They are words of encouragement. Words that helped me overcome my overwhelming anxiety and fear. It is directed to people from all facets of life, so you won't have to live your life simply "pointing and praying." This book is designed to give you the contextual look at these passages, along with the modern application. Whether it is used as a reference guide for discussion, a resource to help a friend or simply a place for you to turn to in times of distress, the main purpose is to help provide you with a Biblical perspective on how to overcome your anxiety and fear.

You do not need to be a slave to your anxiety.

God has a plan for you.

The Old Testament

Exodus

Context- The book of Exodus is the story of the deliverance of the Hebrew people from the tyranny of the Egyptians. The book itself is believed to have been written by Moses. Moses is the man who leads the Israelites in the book of Exodus. God speaks to His people and works miracles through His chosen leader, Moses.

In times of conflict and fear

"Do not be afraid. Stand firm and you will see the deliverance the Lord will bring you today. The Lord will fight for you; you need only to be still." *(Exodus 14:13a,14)*

Modern Application- Fear and panic can create doubt. Those who have faith in God can still feel vulnerable and threatened; panic can be fueled by fear of destruction. It is important to remember that God is in control at all times. He never surrenders control and He saves those who choose to follow Him.

For feelings of unrest, feelings that you have no purpose

"My presence will go with you, and I will give you rest." *(Exodus 33:14)*

Modern Application- You may go about your routines feeling as if you are wandering aimlessly and are without direction. You may also feel as if you are in control of certain aspects of your life, but have no control as to where you will end up. You can envision your goals, or where you would like to be, but struggle with periods of uncertainty as to how you achieve that end. God reminds you that He is always with you. He promises you His rest, when your mind is at the point of its greatest unrest. He will protect you when you allow Him to lead you on the path He has set.

Deuteronomy

Context- Deuteronomy is the final collection of sermons delivered by Moses to the Israelites. After wandering the desert for forty years, a new generation has grown up; ready for God to bring them into the Promised Land. Moses died after delivering the words found in Deuteronomy.

For facing adversity

"Be strong and bold; have no fear or dread of them, because it is the Lord your God who goes before you. He will be with you; he will not fail you or forsake you. Do not fear or be dismayed." *(Deuteronomy 31:6,8)*

Modern Application- God is ahead of you at all times; omnipotent, omniscient, and omnipresent. He is with you, and will not let you down, nor abandon you. You have no reason to fear, or to succumb to mental agitation, or fretting. Remembering God's faithfulness builds your own faith. This faith resonates within you and gives you strength, especially in the face of adversity.

For Support

"The eternal God is your safe place, and underneath are the everlasting arms." *(Deuteronomy 33:27)*

Modern Application- God is everlasting, your protection, and your support for all eternity. God's arms enfold you, holding you close while supporting you.

Joshua

Context- The book of Joshua chronicles the entrance of the Israelites into the Promised Land. The people of Israel had a nomadic history of nearly 200 years, followed by being enslaved by the Egyptians for around 400 years. The Hebrew people were now being led into the land by Joshua, land which they had been promised by God. This land was Canaan, geographically located between Egypt and Mesopotamia. The Israelites were under God's direction to take the land, to destroy the inhabitant cultures. These were pagan cultures centered on the worship of false gods, which included sacrificing their own children.

In times you have fear of the unknown

"Be strong and courageous; do not be frightened or dismayed, for the Lord your God is with you wherever you go." *(Joshua 1:9)*

Modern Application- You are often faced with uncertainty. It is in your nature to go over the "what if's" in your mind. The future is unknown. It is within you to remain strong, have courage, without fear, because God is with you throughout, wherever you go. God promises that He will be your protector; He tells you to have no fear.

Job

Context- The book of Job's author is unknown. What is known is that Job was a God loving man. "Job" has become synonymous with suffering. He was an individual that suffered great losses. He suffered the same difficulties many of us do today. Facing the death of family, loss of his health, and all his material goods, Job rejected much of the reasoning and "advice" he was given by those around him, his friends. Job placed his sufferings before God; questioning why he was being faced with such pain. These sufferings brought before God in the book of Job, are not the isolated complaints of a single individual. Rather, the book of Job takes on the problems that we as *humans* can all identify with throughout our lifetimes. Job tackled many of the questions we ask ourselves. By understanding the book of Job, we can better understand how God is at work within us when we face adversity. We can learn from our difficulties, strengthen our faith and grow within our hearts and minds. By immersing ourselves in God's love, we can better enhance our ability to help those around us who may also be suffering.

In times of doubt

"You will forget your misery; you will remember it as waters that have passed away." *(Job 11:16)*

Modern Application- We are all faced with pain; physically, emotionally, and mentally, in our lives. If you ask forgiveness from God, you will receive, and it will carry into your daily life. Being forthright with God and your mistakes, and if you are willing to receive God's grace, then your period of pain and suffering will pass. The pain you experience may be a result of your mistakes, but you may also be faced with pain at no fault of your own. Although as a human being you do not forget the pain, you remember it as you would a drop of water in a flowing river that is life. Albeit part of life, it becomes a distant and undistinguishable aspect in the grand scheme of existence; possible with God's grace.

In times of loneliness and isolation

"By his light I walked through darkness." *(Job 29:3)*

Modern Application- God is your light in the darkest moments of your life. Feelings of loneliness, emptiness, and isolation are eliminated with the realization that God is always with you, leading you out of the darkness and into the light.

Psalms

Context- Psalms is a book of prayers, mainly written by David, Israel's second king. In line with ancient oral tradition, these prayers were passed from generation to generation through song. The Psalms are not all written in a universal tone. They are prayers written by people who were going through positive times in their lives, and others who were in their darkest hours. They call out respectfully to God; and aim to teach us how to pray openly and honestly.

Finding safety and rest

"I will lie down and sleep in peace, for you alone, O Lord, make me dwell in safety." *(Psalm 4:8)*

Modern Application- You are to rest easy knowing that God protects you. You may worry and contemplate scenarios of troubling events or the unknown future you face, and this may give you anxiety and fear. Sleep easy knowing that God is in control, that you are His, and that He is protecting you.

In times of trouble

"The Lord is a refuge for the oppressed, a stronghold in times of trouble. Those who know your name will trust in you, for you, Lord, have never forsaken those who seek you." *(Psalm 9:9-10)*

Modern Application- *God is your fortress, your safe place in tumultuous times. When confronted with difficult times, ask for His protection. Trust Him. He will never deny those who seek Him. He loves you.*

For support

"I have set the Lord always before me. Because he is at my right hand, I will not be shaken." *(Psalm 16:8)*

Modern Application- Once you know Him, you can be confident that God is always with you. He is even with you during times when you may feel alone. He is with you and will never leave you. Don't be afraid.

Finding joy and comfort

"You show me the path of life. In your presence there is fullness of joy; in your right hand are pleasures forevermore." *(Psalm 16:11)*

Modern Application- When you know Him, God then leads you down a righteous path for the rest of your life. A path that is good! Having Him with you on that path gives you joy and comfort.

A light in the darkness

"It is you who light my lamp; the Lord, my God, lights up my darkness." *(Psalm 18:28)*

Modern Application- God delivers you from the dark times in your life. He gives you hope, and shows you endless love; even when you feel all is lost.

Sustaining you in troubled times

"The Lord is my light and my salvation -- whom shall I fear? The Lord is the stronghold of my life -- of whom shall I be afraid? Though an army besieges me, my heart will not fear; though war break out against me, even then will I be confident. One thing I ask of the Lord, this is what I seek: that I may dwell in the house of the Lord all the days of my life, to gaze upon the beauty of the Lord and to seek him in his temple. For in the day of trouble he will keep me safe in his dwelling; he will hide me in the shelter of his tabernacle and set me high upon a rock." *(Psalm 27:1,3-5)*

Modern Application- God is your light. He is your savior. You have nothing and no one to fear. At times, it may feel as though people are mounting personal attacks on you. You may have an overwhelming sense of rejection, feelings of stress, fear, anxiety, and a desire for isolation. David wanted God more than anything in life and that is just how God wants you to live. Even as the personal storms in life intensify, be **confident** that God, the love of your life, will protect and sustain you.*

Having patience

"Wait for the Lord; be strong, and let your heart take courage; wait for the Lord!" *(Psalm 27:14)*

Modern Application- Ask for and wait for God's grace. Although He is omnipresent and will never abandon you, it is human nature to sometime feel as though you are alone in your trouble. During these times, be strong and take courage and wait. You may not yet know God's plan for you; but you can have faith that He has not abandoned you, because He promised that He would not!

Your protection

"You are my hiding place; you will protect me from trouble and surround me with songs of deliverance." *(Psalm 32:7-8)*

Modern Application- Imagine your worst fear. Now, you have a place to hide from that fear. In your hiding place, you are totally protected from all things that wish to harm you. You can have absolute confidence in this. God is your refuge. In Him you find comfort. He is your protection, and blesses you in a multitude of ways; day and night.

Freedom from your fear

"I sought the Lord, and he answered me, and delivered me from all my fears." *(Psalm 34:4)*

Modern Application- David was delivered from all his fears because He took his fears to the Lord and the Lord answered his prayer. You can experience God in exactly the same way. In times of trouble, it may feel as though God is nowhere to be found. This is not the case. You simply need to seek Him; He will be found. God's presence alone delivers you from anxiety.

Knowing you are never alone- An extra measure of help

"The angel of the Lord encamps around those who fear him, and delivers them." *(Psalm 34:7)*

Modern Application- There are angels protecting and fighting for those who know and follow God—yet another reason why you can let go of your feelings of overwhelming stress, fear, or anxiety . There's a lot going on that we can't see, and this is another promise of God's deliverance.

Pursuing what is good

"Those who seek the Lord lack no good thing." *(Psalm 34:10b)*

Modern Application- Those who are seeking God, are seeking good. During times of high stress, fear, or anxiety you may often feel down on yourself, amplifying your failures in your mind. Temporary solutions, vices, do not deliver you from your troubles. But those who are truly seeking God have no room for ungodly solutions. You are to seek protection, and deliverance from persistent negative thoughts and emotions; trusting in the eternal God who will deliver you from these anxieties, because of the love He has for you.

In troubled times

"When the righteous cry for help, the Lord hears, and rescues them from all their troubles. The Lord is near to the brokenhearted, and saves the crushed in spirit. Many are the afflictions of the righteous, but the Lord rescues them from them all." *(Psalm 34:17-19)*

Modern Application- If you trust in God, and cry out for help, you are not only heard, but delivered from your troubles. God is close when you are hurting. He saves those who feel as if they are at the end of their rope.

Having faith

"Trust in the Lord and do good; so you will live in the land, and enjoy security. Take delight in the Lord and he will give you the desires of your heart. Commit your way to the Lord; trust in him, and he will act. Be still before the Lord, and wait patiently for him."
(Psalm 37:3-5, 7a)

Modern Application- (You are to have faith in God, and live according to His word daily. This better enables you to relax and live justly for God. You are not perfect, and you need to open up to God.) When you seek God in prayer, silence your heart and mind to the surrounding world and you'll become more open and focused. Pray honestly and wait patiently; God hears your prayers. He will protect you and deliver you from your anxieties. Trust God enough to take a few risks--risk doing what is good, not just what's right, but what's good for others. You will enjoy secure living—the desire of your anxious heart.

In chaotic times

"Why are you cast down, O my soul, and why are you disquieted within me? Hope in God; for I shall again praise him, my help and my God... By day the Lord commands his steadfast love, and at night his song is with me, a prayer to the God of my life." *(Psalm 42: 5,8)*

Modern Application- We all experience times when we feel broken and beaten down by the stresses we experience. During these difficult periods, choose to hope, that is trust in God. He will rebuild and refine you. Day and night, at all times God is with you with His everlasting love. He puts an end to the chaos.

Strength in safety

"God is our refuge and strength, an ever-present help in trouble. Therefore we will not fear, though the earth give way and the mountains fall into the heart of the sea, though its waters roar and foam and the mountains quake with their surging." *(Psalm 46:1-3)*

Modern Application- God is your protection in a seemingly chaotic world. At times, you may feel as though the world is crashing all around you. It is during these tumultuous times that you can have confidence that God is your protection and source of strength. He is omnipresent with an everlasting love that overcomes.

Putting your anxiety to rest

"Be still, and know that I am God." *(Psalm 46:10a)*

*Modern Application- You can put all of your stress, fear and anxiety to rest. God is the God of the universe; everlasting, all powerful and full of love. Know that the God of all loves you. God is in **total** control and you can rest assured He will protect and sustain you. Your anxieties, initially at the forefront of your mind, are miniscule in comparison to the good God has planned for you.*

Getting past your past

"Create in me a clean heart, O God, and put a new and right spirit within me. Do not cast me from your presence or take your Holy Spirit from me. Restore to me the joy of your salvation, and grant me a willing spirit, to sustain me." *(Psalm 51:10-12)*

Modern Application- You are imperfect. We are all sinners. Even the most pious and God-loving falter and offend Him. You may regret things you have done, and feel as though you will never be forgiven. If you continue in your walk with God, even when you do stumble, and ask sincerely for His forgiveness, God restores you. He does so despite your shortcomings; out of love. He will deliver you from your torments, and restore your confidence in His love that we all so desperately need.

In times of loneliness

"Hear my cry, O God; listen to my prayer. From the ends of the earth I call to you, I call as my heart grows faint; lead me to the rock that is higher than I. For you have been my refuge, a strong tower against the foe. I long to dwell in your tent forever and take refuge in the shelter of your wings." *(Psalm 61:1-4)*

Modern Application- You may feel anxiety and a sense of deep-rooted loneliness in your dark hours. No matter what the situation, remember the love God has shown you. Pray to Him in those dark times. Take shelter in His love. These negative thoughts and fears will not hold firm in your mind and heart. There is peace and security in God.

For protection

"My soul finds rest in God alone; my salvation comes from him. He alone is my rock and my salvation; he is my fortress, I will never be shaken." *(Psalm 62:1-2)*

Modern Application- You can find solace in God. In accepting Him, you are saved, and delivered from sin. There is no weakness in this, and you cannot be shaken, because you are protected. Your eternity is secure!

Building your foundation

"Be thou my strong habitation, whereunto I may continually resort: thou has given commandment to save me; for thou art my rock and my fortress." *(Psalm 71:3; KJV)*

Modern Application- *You can ask God for help. You can ask God to protect you during times of turmoil. You pray: He does listen. Your relationship with God is an everlasting relationship built on a solid foundation.*

Finding restoration

"Though you have made me see troubles, many and bitter, you will restore my life again; from the depths of the earth you will again bring me up." *(Psalm 71:20)*

Modern Application- You are exposed to pain and hurt. You experience events that trouble, scar, and have the potential to ruin you. You hear, see, read, and experience things that stay with you, that replay in your mind and would damage your heart. Trust God to restore you. He will demonstrate His love, and make you whole again. He will pick you up.

Building yourself up with what really matters

"My flesh and my heart may fail, but God is the strength of my heart and my portion forever." (Psalm 73:26)

Modern Application- You stumble from time to time in your life. God sees this, but remains with you throughout; and loves you despite your shortcomings. Your body ages, and it will not last you for an eternity. God is your strength that will not weaken with time. It will survive for eternity.

For strength

"Blessed are those whose strength is in you, who have set their hearts on pilgrimage. They go from strength to strength, till each appears before God in Zion." *(Psalm 84:5,7)*

Modern Application- Those who accept God into their lives are truly blessed. As you walk with God day-to-day, you experience bumps in the road. This does not mean your walk ends. You grow more and more in Him as you cooperate with God's plan for your life. Your life continues, walking while protected by God, until your time ends and you see the true glory of God in heaven.

Having confidence

"You who live in the shelter of the Most High, who abide in the shadow of the Almighty, will say to the Lord, "My refuge and my fortress; my God in whom I trust."" *(Psalm 91:1-2)*

Modern Application- If you live in God's presence, and that is a choice you make, you can have confidence in His protection. Tell Him that you trust Him to keep you safe.

Protection from your fears

""Those who love me, I will deliver; I will protect those who know my nature" says God. "When they call to me, I will answer them; I will be with them in trouble, I will rescue them and honor them. With long life I will satisfy them, and show them my salvation."" *(Psalm 91:14-16)*

Modern Application- God promises you that He is with you at all times! He hears your prayers. It is for those who love Him and know Him. He stands by you in your times of trouble. In times of high anxiety and fear, God is your protection!

Replacing anxiety with joy

"When I said, "My foot is slipping," your love, O Lord, supported me. When anxiety was great within me, your consolation brought joy to my soul." *(Psalm 94:18-19)*

Modern Application- *You may feel as though you are targeted by others. Others attempt to tear you down, and you may be dumbfounded as to how or why these things are directed at you. God is not the cause of these actions. He is however your support in times of trouble. He is with you during those difficult times. He hears your desire to be free from the pain, free from the rejection, and free from the anxiety that accompanies it. Even when it feels as though there is nobody standing by you and you are alone, God is there. He loves you throughout, delivers you from your struggles, and brings you joy through His love.*

Finding acceptance

"Bless the Lord, O my soul, and do not forget all his benefits—who forgives all your sins and heals all your diseases, who redeems your life from the pit and crowns you with love and compassion, who satisfies your desires with good things so that your youth is renewed like the eagle's." *(Psalm 103:2-5)*

Modern Application- God forgives you for all things if you can accept Jesus into your heart. In your life, as time goes on, you can feel beaten and bruised, worn down and helpless. Through Jesus your sins are forgiven. You are cleansed from your shortcomings. In His eyes you are renewed, reborn, loved!

Becoming free from fear with a strong heart and mind

"Praise the Lord! Happy are those who fear the Lord... They are not afraid of evil tidings; their hearts are firm, secure in the Lord. Their hearts are steady, they will not be afraid." *(Psalm 112:1a,7-8a)*

Modern Application- In accepting God, you can be renewed. This enables you to put all fear aside; not succumbing to the evil things you are exposed to daily. Your heart can be strong and your soul grounded, because you are secure in your faith. With this comes fearlessness. The petty things that give you anxiety that you naturally want to control but cannot, no longer have the same influence on you as they once did. The reason for this is that you know you are loved, and protected by the God of all things.

Finding rest

"Be at rest once more, O my soul, for the Lord has been good to you. For you, O Lord, have delivered my soul from death, my eyes from tears, my feet from stumbling, that I may walk before the Lord in the land of the living." *(Psalm 116:7-9)*

Modern Application- It is important for you to realize that God has truly blessed you in your life, even if it does not seem so at times. When surrounded by negativity, if you only focus on the bad, you will not acknowledge the blessings at all. If you can have a grateful heart, reflect and realize the ways in which you have been blessed, you can know the things God has done for you; and begin to experience God's love day-to-day. He has delivered you from pain before, shown you happy times, and will do so again if you simply cultivate a grateful spirit and allow Him to.

Sustaining you despite your mistakes

"I will not die but live, and will proclaim what the Lord has done. The Lord has chastened me severely, but he has not given me over to death." *(Psalm 118:17-18)*

Modern Application- You are tested and you do fail at times. You may despair and want to give up, but realize God never gives up on you. He has a plan for you, and loves you unconditionally.

When feeling defeated

"My soul is weary with sorrow; strengthen me according to your word." *(Psalm 119:28)*

Modern Application- You may often feel tired or beat mentally, emotionally, and spiritually. You can pray and God will hear those prayers. Immerse yourself in God's Word; His promises are a source of strength.

In times of suffering

"My comfort in my suffering is this: Your promise preserves my life." *(Psalm 119:50)*

Modern Application- You suffer at times. Be comforted by God's love and promise of deliverance, and you will persevere.

Eliminating your fear and undo stress

"Unless the Lord builds the house, those who build it labor in vain. Unless the Lord guards the city, the guard keeps watch in vain. It is in vain that you rise up early and go late to rest, eating the bread of anxious toil; for he gives sleep to his beloved." *(Psalm 127:1-2)*

Modern Application- If you do not build your faith and maintain your spirit in God, you are living beyond your means. God is the foundation by which you need to build, in order to sustain yourself. If you try to control all things, things that give us anxiety, you will most likely become overextended and worn down.

The breeding ground of anxiety is striving to accomplish something as though its success depends on us, when, in fact, it doesn't depend on us at all. God is in every detail of the lives of His beloved. We can sleep confidently knowing that it's all in good hands. Like a newborn- babies can't do a thing for themselves; they simply trust, and they sleep soundly.

In times of need

"When I called, you answered me; you made me bold and stouthearted." *(Psalm 138:3)*

Modern Application- God answers you- in accordance with His plan for you. You are to have courage! He shows you His support; which enables you to have confidence.

Protection from trouble

"Though I walk in the midst of trouble, you preserve my life; you stretch out your hand against the anger of my foes, with your right hand you save me." *(Psalm 138:7)*

Modern Application- You may be confronted with difficulty, and often see stressful situations looming. Remember this image of God's strong right hand reaching in to save you. God is actively saving you from troublesome situations.

For your anxious thoughts, finding guidance

"Where can I go from your Spirit? Where can I flee from your presence? If I rise on the wings of the dawn, if I settle on the far side of the sea, even there your hand will guide me, your right hand will hold me fast. If I say, "Surely the darkness will hide me and the light become night around me," even the darkness will not be dark to you; the night will shine like the day, for darkness is as light to you. Search me, O God, and know my heart; test me and know my anxious thoughts. See if there is any offensive way in me, and lead me in the way everlasting." *(Psalm 139:7,9-12,23-24)*

Modern Application- You can know that God is everywhere and that He does not ever abandon you. He will guide you at all times in life, good and bad. Much as you may feel that darkness and negativity may be closing in all around you, God is there. Seek the light of God. God destroys darkness and reveals His light. You can ask God to take the anxious thoughts that are within you and destroy them completely, delivering you from your anxiety.

In fearful times

"My eyes are fixed on you, O Sovereign Lord; in you I take refuge--do not give me over to death." *(Psalm 141:8)*

Modern Application- Take solace in God's love, power and presence. Do not take your eyes off God. He will never abandon you.

Sincerity in your need

"The Lord is near to all who call on him, to all who call on him in truth. He fulfills the desires of those who fear him; he hears their cry and saves them." *(Psalm 145: 18-19)*

Modern Application- God hears all prayers. He comes close to those who are truly sincere in their prayers. He can tell the difference between prayers that are made with conviction, and those that are half-hearted. He knows all things. God can distinguish those who truly want Him from those who don't. He won't deny you when you are sincere and honest in your desire for His closeness.

When feeling broken

"He heals the brokenhearted, and binds up their wounds." *(Psalm 147:3)*

Modern Application- God knows your hurt. He is your healer. Much like dressing a series of deep cuts, God takes care of each and every injury you have to your soul with surgical precision. No injury goes ignored or untreated.

Proverbs

Context- The book of Proverbs is mainly written by King Solomon; David's successor. Solomon was widely known for his wealth and wisdom. The book is a book of wisdom. The wisdom Solomon writes about pertains to how we live our lives and not necessarily how book-smart an individual may be. These writings of Solomon are classified by theme rather then context, because there is no time and place to the passages themselves. The people of Solomon's time struggled with much of the same issues we face today. The

Proverbs are just as true today as they were the day they were written; and are just as helpful in our world.

Admitting you do not have all the answers

"Trust in the Lord with all your heart and lean not on your own understanding; in all your ways acknowledge him, and he will make your paths straight." *(Proverbs 3:5-6)*

Modern Application- *Have faith and trust that God will lead you. Often you may try to assess and figure out every situation that arises in your life. If you can make God your source of right living, you can then stand firm in that God will lead you in the right direction. This ends your stress and anxiety in a world of uncertainty.*

For a restless mind

"When you lie down, you will not be afraid; when you lie down, your sleep will be sweet." *(Proverbs 3:24)*

Modern Application- You may often lie down to sleep replaying the stresses of the day in your mind. You may also attempt to rehearse the hypothetical situations you see arising in the day (or days) to come. Often, you may go over the "worst-case scenarios" you see that may arise. Understand that the future is unknown and you cannot control every aspect of what is to come. God tells you that when you rest you should not fear what is to come, because He is in **total** *control. He instructs you to rest easy, rest well, and give all of our anxieties to Him. He can handle anything you are faced with. He will deal with your struggles according to His plan for you.*

Knowing you are safe

"The name of the Lord is a strong tower; the righteous run into it and are safe." *(Proverbs 18:10)*

Modern Application- You can find solace in God's strength. Run to Him. He protects you.

Your safety in God

"Fear of others will prove to be a snare, but whoever trusts in the Lord is kept safe." *(Proverbs 29:25)*

Modern Application- Stress, fear, and anxiety of what people say and do behind your back can cripple you. Constant worry and fear about others' opinions of you can give you extreme anxiety and directly affect your personal, professional, and social life. Constant mental torment in this regard can even affect the way in which you view yourself. The constant fear of being viewed in a negative light wears you down mentally and emotionally. Trust God and you can overcome this. Know God is your protector. Experiencing God's love first hand is the end of anxiety!

Isaiah

Context- The Book of Isaiah was written by the prophet Isaiah. Isaiah was a smart man from a well off and presumably influential family in Judah. He encountered God's glory and was called by God to prophesy. The book focuses on how God is with us and how he uses each and every experience of our lives, both good and bad.

God is your strength

""Surely God is my salvation; I will trust and not be afraid. The Lord, the Lord, is my strength and my song; he has become my salvation". With joy you will draw water from the wells of salvation." *(Isaiah 12:2)*

Modern Application- Be joyful that God can rescue you from your difficulties! He does not always change the circumstances. He has something better in mind for you! God is in control.

For trusting God

"Those of steadfast mind you keep in peace—because they trust in you. Trust in the Lord forever,

for in the Lord God you have an everlasting rock."
(Isaiah 26: 3-4)

Modern Application- You are able to keep a level head, free of panic when you trust in God. He never leaves you! He gives you peace that will last for eternity. Trust in God; God will build you up. You have a strong foundation by which you can share your life with others.

Finding peace

"Lord, you establish peace for us; all that we have accomplished you have done for us." *(Isaiah 26:12)*

Modern Application- God wants you to live at peace. He gives you that peace.

Acknowledging your faults, and trust in God

"In repentance and rest is your salvation, in quietness and trust is your strength." *(Isaiah 30:15)*

Modern Application- Much of your stress and anxiety comes from the fear of the unknown, loss of control, fear of losing control, or simply being in situations you would rather avoid. You may want to **plan** *and have everything in line with what you want. This however is not always possible and raises fears within you as a result. God instructs you to simply let go of this need for control, ask for forgiveness for your sins, and take peace in knowing that you are forgiven in accepting Him. In doing this, God makes you aware that you will no longer have these unwarranted,* *sometimes irrational, anxious moments. Your anxiety becomes quieted when you know you are in a relationship with God. You become settled and stronger in your heart and mind; deriving strength from the grace God has shown you.*

For a fearful heart

"Say to those with fearful hearts, "Be strong, do not fear; your God will come, he will come with vengeance; with divine retribution he will come to save you."" *(Isaiah 35:4-5)*

Modern Application- At times you are forced to be silent, unable to speak up for yourself or defend those you would like to defend in fear of rejection or retribution. This can cause great levels of anxiety within you. God tells you that it these scenarios will come and you are not to become fearful, anxious, or stressed from these situations. You are to rest knowing that God sees these things. He knows the issues and frustrations in your heart. Put your faith in God that He will protect and sustain you. Have faith that God will address the issues you face. His plan is your good.

For feelings of brokenness

"Do you not know? Have you not heard? The Lord is the everlasting God, the Creator of the ends of the earth. He will not grow tired or weary, and His understanding no one can fathom. He gives strength to the weary and increases the power of the weak. Even youths grow tired and weary, and young men stumble and fall; but those who hope in the Lord will renew their strength. They will soar on wings like eagles; they will run and not grow weary, they will walk and not be faint." *(Isaiah 40:28-31)*

Modern Application- God is the Creator of all things. He is everlasting and all knowing. Sometimes you may feel worn down and beaten. God sees this and knows your troubles. He reminds you that even the strongest feel tired at times. The wisest have felt dismayed and beaten as well. You are not alone in these struggles. Through God, you can be rebuilt and rejuvenated. God promises that if you walk with Him, you can and will overcome what ever weighs heavy on your heart and mind. You can rest easy knowing He is looking out for you.

When you feel down

"So do not fear, for I am with you; do not be dismayed, for I am your God. I will strengthen you and help you; I will uphold you with my righteous right hand." *(Isaiah 41:10)*

Modern Application- *God tells you not to be fearful. You have no need to panic. He tells you that you are not alone. He is always with you, even when you feel isolated. He strengthens you while protecting you. He upholds you, and builds you up in your broken state. Have no fear, because you know that the God of all things is in control.*

In difficult times

"Do not fear, for I have redeemed you; I have called you by name, you are mine. When you pass through the waters, I will be with you; and through the rivers, they shall not overwhelm you; when you walk through fire you shall not be burned, and the flame shall not consume you. For I am the Lord your God, the Holy One of Israel, your Savior." *(Isaiah 43:1b-3a)*

Modern Application- God tells the redeemed, those who belong to Him, not to fear. You belong to Him for all eternity, and you should not fear anything in the moment, because God is in total control. When you feel overwhelmed by your family, stress in your personal relationships, your career, your health, or even things you can't seem to get over in your past, it can feel as if you are drowning; helpless and living in torment with no end in sight. Although it may not be apparent to others, you may struggle with this state of being daily. God knows this, claims you as His own and tells you not to fear. He does not wish for you to live this way, and is your Savior who delivers you from these fears and gives you relief from your internal, daily struggles.

For comfort

"As a mother comforts her child, so will I comfort you." (Isaiah 66:13a)

Modern Application- God will bring you comfort. The image of a mother comforting her child is powerful, probably the most powerful comparison in our human understanding.

Jeremiah

Context- Jeremiah was called by God to be His prophet at a young age. Jeremiah wrote between 650- 580 B.C. God revealed to Jeremiah that the nation of Judah would fall due to their disobedience to God. As difficult times plagued the nation, the preaching of Jeremiah was not well received. He was persecuted, threatened, and ridiculed by the people for what He preached. He was able to maintain his faith, overcoming adversity, because he knew God was protecting Him. He was preaching what God had revealed to Him. A major lesson of the book of Jeremiah is that even in times of distress, when our world seems to be crumbling before our eyes, God has a plan for us, and it is for our good, even if we cannot see or understand His purposes yet. He loves us, protects us, and will guide us through difficult times.

For safety and trust

"O Lord, my strength and my fortress, my refuge in time of distress." *(Jeremiah 16:19)*

Modern Application- Faith in God that He is your protection gives you strength. Tell God you trust Him to care for you, and you will receive his reassurance. In anxious times, you can derive strength in knowing that He is your protector.

In times of uncertainty- an honest search

""For I know the plans I have for you," declares the Lord, "plans to prosper you and not to harm you, plans to give you hope and a future. Then you will call upon me and come and pray to me, and I will listen to you. You will seek me and find me when you seek me with all your heart. I will be found by you," declares the Lord, "and will bring you back from captivity.""
(Jeremiah 29:11-14a)

Modern Application- You may often find yourself in uncomfortable and unfamiliar circumstances. These scenarios can give you extreme amounts of stress, fear, and anxiety whether it is a result of the choices you have made or simply that you find yourself thrust into circumstances by forces beyond your control. This can make you feel as though you are a prisoner; crippled and crushed by your circumstances. God tells you that in these instances, if you truly seek His guidance, you will find Him. God will help you through your difficulties. God will not abandon those who are honest in their search for Him. Not only will He give you comfort, but He will rescue you.

In times of loneliness

"I have loved you with an everlasting love; I have drawn you to myself you with loving-kindness." *(Jeremiah 31:3)*

Modern Application- God has loved you, and will continue to love you no matter what. You are by His design. Even in times of loneliness, when you feel unhappy in your own skin, God tells you that He made you in His image with an everlasting love. He loved you before you before you even existed. Remember that when feeling loved doesn't come easy.

For facing adversity

"See, I am the Lord, the God of all mankind; is anything too hard for me?" *(Jeremiah 32:27)*

Modern Application- Jeremiah prophesized that the mighty city would fall to the Babylonians. What God intends to do, He is able to do. You may often feel as though your own life is on the brink of collapse. You may feel anxious, mentally and emotionally exhausted, and at a loss as to what you can do about your circumstances. God wants you to know that you do not have to crumble. God wants you to give Him your burdens, because there is nothing He cannot handle. God is in control, so you have no need to fear anything.

Lamentations

Context- The author of Lamentations is not known, but it may have been written by the prophet Jeremiah. After the fall of Jerusalem, destroyed by the Babylonians in 586 BC, God's people suffered immensely.

In times of suffering, doubt, loneliness, restlessness

"Because of the Lord's great love we are not consumed, for his compassions never fail. They are new every morning; great is your faithfulness. I say to myself, "The Lord is my portion; therefore I will wait for him." The Lord is good to those whose hope is in him, to the one who seeks him; it is good to wait quietly for the salvation of the Lord." *(Lamentations 3:22-26)*

Modern Context- God's love will never fail you. It is human to feel lonely at times. Everyone experiences heartache and pain. God tells you that it is good to long for Him. God wants you to wait patiently, to pray, and to seek Him with all your heart in times of distress. He has not abandoned you, He does hear your prayers, and He will save you from your troubles when the time is right. While it may be difficult to do, you are to persevere, and wait for God to act in your life.

For times you feel targeted

"For the Lord will not reject forever. Although he causes grief, he will have compassion according to the abundance of his steadfast love; for he does not willingly afflict or grieve anyone." *(Lamentations 3:31-32)*

Modern Context- God has compassion for you, and that is the reason you experience what you do. We all experience times in our lives when we may believe things could not go any worse. God knows the things that are in your mind and heart. He has compassion for you. He loves you even in your darkest hour.

Micah

Context- Micah writes about the presence of God in our world. He gives a unique account of God, because he does not write about the physical world, and where God fits in. Rather, Micah writes about God's presence in us, and where God makes His presence known by our sense of His love. Micah prophesied between 740 and 690 B.C. This is presumably just after the foundation of Rome.

For times you feel broken

"Do not rejoice over me, O my enemy; when I fall, I shall rise; when I sit in darkness, the Lord will be a light to me." *(Micah 7:8)*

Modern Application- *When you feel beaten and broken by those who are seemingly out to get you for their own personal gain, you are **not** in fact beaten and broken. Although you may feel stressed, fearful, and full of anxiety, God is your guardian. God is more powerful than any person, and will prevail in His own way; He will demonstrate His love for you in the process.*

Zephaniah

Context- The prophet Zephaniah was a well connected man of influence, highly regarded in the political system of his time (635-625 B.C.). He wrote of the connection between all people and God. Zephaniah wrote during a time of revival for Israel.

For times you need compassion

"The Lord your God is with you, he is mighty to save. He will take great delight in you, he will quiet you with his love, he will rejoice over you with singing." *(Zephaniah 3:17)*

Modern Application- God is always with you, and He is powerful. He takes joy in your successes, and in your personal growth when you fail. He takes pleasure in calming your spirit amidst worry. He wants you to succeed. Allow Him to silence your anxieties.

Nehemiah (included in Ezra)

Context- After the 70 years of captivity in Babylon, God's people were allowed to return to their land to rebuild. Nehemiah supervised the reconstruction of the walls of Jerusalem under the direction of Ezra, a religious scholar.

For times of grief

"Do not grieve, for the joy of the Lord is your strength." *(Nehemiah 8:10b)*

Modern Application- In times of grief and high tension, you may often feel compelled to sulk and despair when you feel all is lost. God does not want you to feel this way. He instructs you to celebrate Him; and demonstrate your joy to others. You are not alone in your struggles. He hears your cries for help, and will help you. Joy comes from knowing that the all powerful God of the universe is in control. You have no need to grieve, you can be strong.

The New Testament

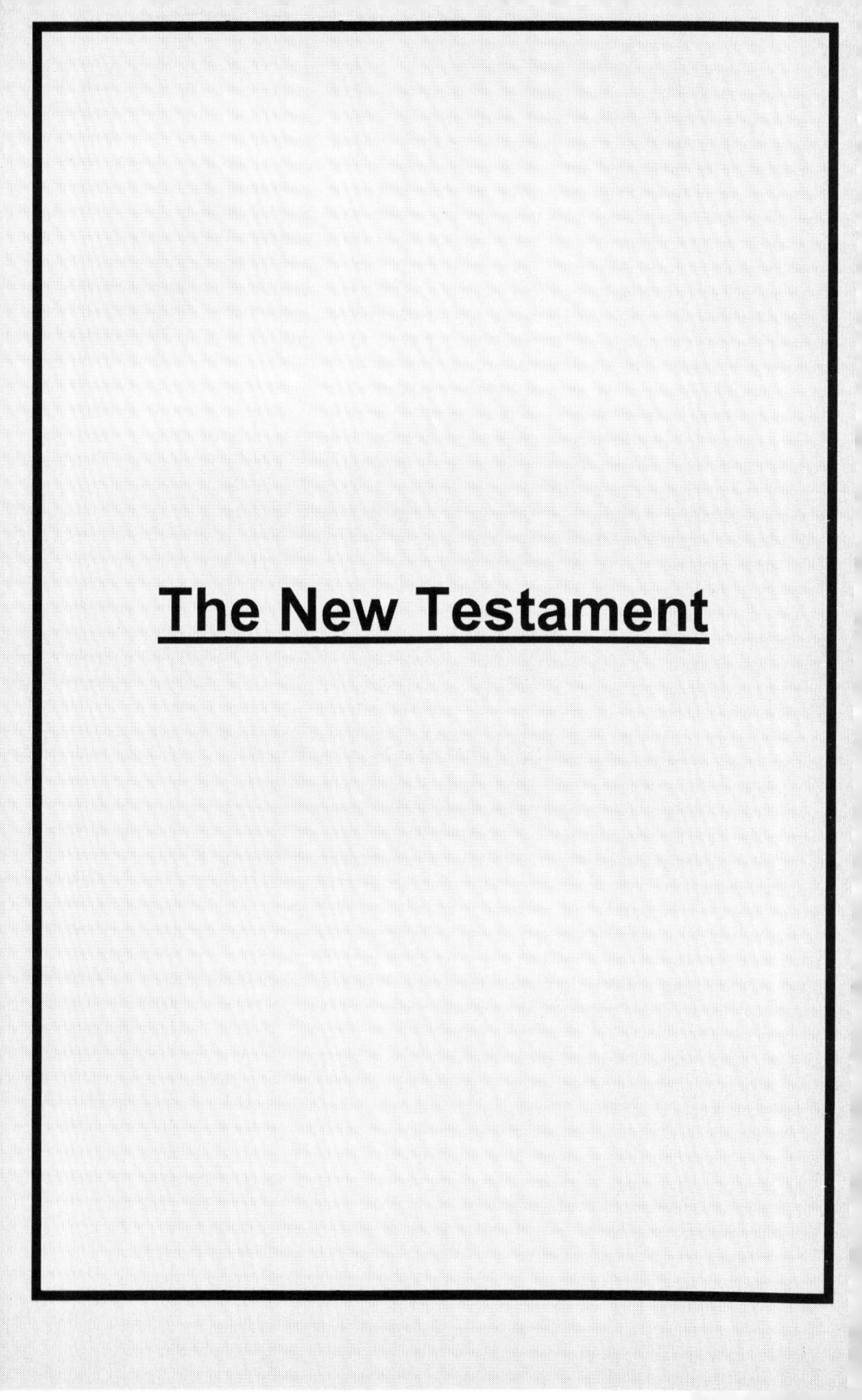

Matthew

Context- Matthew wrote the first gospel—an account of the life and teachings of Jesus Christ. He was one of the twelve apostles, so he knew the Lord personally. The selected texts are Jesus' own words.

Times of worry, fear, and anxiety

"Your father knows what you need before you ask him. So do not worry, saying 'What shall we eat?' or 'What shall we wear?' For the pagans run after all these things, and your heavenly Father knows that you need them. But seek first his kingdom and his righteousness, and all these things will be given to you as well. Therefore do not worry about tomorrow, for tomorrow will worry about itself. Today's trouble is enough for today." *(Matthew 6:8b, 31-34)*

*Modern Application- Jesus **knew** of **your** day-to-day anxieties. He assures you that the Father knows all of it! Your fears, both founded and unfounded can trigger anxiety, doubt, and even panic attacks. You attempt to control them, but can not stop these panic-inducing thoughts as hard as you may try.*

Jesus knew this and spoke of how you can conquer these fears. He reassures you and wants you to seek God, and give Him your worry. You live in the present, and the future is unknown. God is in control of all things and He wants you to have faith in Him in your present situations. Jesus said you are to maintain your faith that God is in control of your future and there is no need to fear.

For lightening your burdens, finding rest

"Come to me, all you who are weary and burdened, and I will give you rest. Take my yoke upon you and learn from me, for I am gentle and humble in heart, and you will find rest for your souls. For my yoke is easy and my burden is light." *(Matthew 11: 28-31)*

Modern Application- Jesus was encouraging those who felt broken and beaten down to come to Him, to surrender to Him. He is your strength. He leads you. When stress, fear, and anxiety wear you down, Jesus tells you that God will give you rest. Jesus encourages you to trust Him. Accept God's grace. Your burdens of stress, fear, and anxiety are lifted.

Finding trust, even for things beyond your control

"If you have faith the size of a mustard seed, you will say to this mountain, "move from here to there," and it will move; and nothing will be impossible for you." (Matthew 17:20)

Modern Application- When you are suffering from stress, fear, or anxiety, you may feel as though nothing is possible; helpless and hopeless. Jesus tells you that anything is possible when you have faith in God. You need not fear anything when you have faith; all things are possible through Him.

Luke

Context- Luke's writing was based on eyewitness accounts of those who knew Jesus. He was a well versed doctor; who knew Greek. He wrote in a conversational fashion that could reach a huge demographic. Luke wanted to communicate the message Jesus was teaching that *everyone* is offered a place in God's kingdom. No person was excluded based on race, sex, position or mistakes made in their past. All were welcome who come to a saving relationship with Jesus.

Knowing you matter

"Are not five sparrows sold for two pennies? Yet not one of them is forgotten in God's sight. But even the hairs of your head are all counted. Do not be afraid; you are of more value than many sparrows." *(Luke 12:6-7)*

Modern Application- God is the creator of all things. Jesus taught that God knows everything there is to know about you. Of all of His creations on earth, God values people the most—we are made in His image. He reminds you not to fear, because He knows you, He loves you and He will take care of you.

Eliminating worry

"Can any of you by worrying add a single hour to your span of life? If then you are not able to do so small a thing as that, why do you worry about the rest." *(Luke 12:25-26)*

Modern Application- Jesus reminds you that there are things in your life that you cannot control. Worry, fear, and anxiety don't change that. It is then up to you to recognize that God is in control of all things. If you are able identify the things that are out of your control, give your anxieties to God, then you need not have fear of those things any longer.

Eliminating fear

"Do not be afraid, little flock, for it is your Father's good pleasure to give you the kingdom." *(Luke 12:32)*

Modern Application- It is not uncommon to worry about day-to-day things; trouble at work, at home, financial obligations, or anything else that gives us heightened levels of stress. Jesus instructs you should not be fearful. Heightened instances of worry can paralyze you and make you unaware of the way God is working in your life. Accept God's grace and rest assured that He will take care of you. He has a plan for your good. God's children are in good hands; well protected and cared for.

John

Context- John, the author of this gospel, was a beloved apostle of Jesus. An eyewitness to Jesus' ministry, crucifixion, death, and resurrection, he wrote that Jesus is the *living* Son of God, that He was sent from Heaven to save us from our sins, and that He is the Messiah that had been prophesized to forever change the world.

Finding peace

"Peace I leave with you; my peace I give you. I do not give to you as the world gives. Do not let your hearts be troubled and do not be afraid. "*(John 14:27)*

Modern Application- *You may often suffer immense feelings of loneliness, rejection, or a sense of impending suffering that you can see coming, but cannot control or stop. Often, you may try to promise yourself that you will not let these situations cripple you, because you tell yourself you are a strong individual. Jesus reminds you that God is in control. You are in fact never alone, never rejected, if you are grounded in His love. There is nothing on this earth that can give you peace like God's love. You are not to fear, because God is in control. His love for you is everlasting. Accept it.*

Finding your place, building your life in His love

"Abide in me as I abide in you. Just as the branch cannot bear fruit by itself unless it abides in the vine, neither can you unless you abide in me. I am the vine, you are the branches. Those who abide in me and I in them bear much fruit, because apart from me you can do nothing. If you abide in me, and my words abide in you, ask for whatever you wish, and it will be done for you. If you keep my commandments, you will abide in my love, just as I have kept my Father's commandments and abide in his love." *(John 15:4-5,7,10)*

Modern Application- *You may often try to do too much. As a result you can become overly stressed. Jesus reminds you that if you are not grounded in Him, you will accomplish nothing of kingdom value. Too often you may ask for help when you are at your wits end, your breaking point. When you ask God for help, He is ready and willing, and pleasures in doing so. But remember that God's willingness to act on our behalf is sometimes predicated on our obedience to His word. If we belong to Him, we will want to please Him by obeying His word.*

Romans

Context- Paul wrote this letter to the believers in Rome around three decades after the resurrection of Jesus Christ. Paul was an educated man who devoted his life to spreading the message of Jesus throughout the Roman Empire.

A positive outlook on things to come

"I consider that the sufferings of this present time are not worth comparing with the glory about to be revealed to us." *(Romans 8:18)*

Modern Application- Stress, fear, and anxiety are culmination of your thoughts, dwelling on difficulties you currently face, or believe you will face in the future. If you are able to get past your present difficulties, acknowledge that the future is unknown, and take a look at what Jesus has done for you in the grand scheme, then you have no reason for worry. The troubles you know and the pain you have experienced do not define you. You are a child of God and will experience His glory! You do have a glorious future with Him!

Allowing God to work in your life

"And we know that in all things God works for the good of those who love him, who have been called according to his purpose." *(Romans 8:28)*

Modern Application- Accepting Jesus' gift of salvation and inviting God's Holy Spirit into your heart does not make you impervious to the stresses of your world. God knows your heart and mind. He knows when you are stressed, fearful, and anxious. Know that God is working to help you through difficult times, because He takes an active role in your life (He lives with you, after all!), and wants to protect you. He has a purpose for you. His purpose for you is in accordance with His plan; and His plan is good!

The greatest gift for you

"If God is for us, who can be against us? Who shall separate us from the love of Christ? Shall trouble or hardship or persecution or famine or nakedness or danger or sword? No, in all these things we are more than conquerors through Him who loved us. For I am convinced that neither death nor life, neither angels nor demons, neither the present nor the future, nor any powers, neither height nor depth, nor anything else in all creation, will be able to separate us from the love of God that is in Christ Jesus our Lord." *(Romans 8:31b,35,37-39)*

*Modern Application- There is **nothing** that can undo what Jesus did for you. God giving His son was the ultimate sacrifice. When accepting what Jesus did for you and inviting God into your heart, **completely** forgiving you for your sins, you can be reborn. Stress, fear, and anxiety are results of doubt, uncertainty, or lack of control. God knows the things that weigh you down. Have faith that He can eliminate all doubt within you if you can simply trust Him, because He has all the answers. Your choices can separate you from God. Accepting what Christ did for you on the cross, bridges the gap of this separation. It brings you back to God. He is in **total** control.*

For resisting temptation, deception

"The God of peace will soon crush Satan under your feet." *(Romans 16:20)*

Modern Application- Stress, fear, and anxiety can be brought on by things you feel you cannot stop. In accepting God's love, you can rest assured that in due time God will eliminate the fear and doubt that seek to control you and give you undo stress. If you fully envelope yourself in God's love, He can conquer anything that seeks to destroy you. Satan's days are numbered. You will be rid of his diabolical schemes against you once and for all. And in the meantime, God will give you victory against his schemes.

1 Corinthians

Context- After receiving the call of God to take the gospel to the world, Paul established the church in Corinth. These were new believers living in a pagan culture. Paul then left to teach elsewhere. In time, he received notice that the pagan culture was seeping back into this congregation. This letter to the Corinthians was written with firmness but compassion to reestablish what that had learned prior.

You are not alone in your troubles

"No testing has overtaken you that is not common to everyone. God is faithful, and he will not let you be tested beyond your strength, but with the testing he will also provide the way out so that you may be able to endure it." *(1 Corinthians 10:13)*

Modern Application- Often in times of high stress and anxiety you may feel as though the situation is yours and yours alone. This is not the case. There is someone at some point in history, if not at that very same moment, that has gone or is going through the same stress. God knows what you are going through. You are not alone in your struggles. God is there for you and is in total control of all things. He does not throw you into situations that you can not handle with Him. He knows your limits *and your breaking points. He does not surpass those limits; so trust in Him. As you are faced with struggles, God always provides an escape route-- the means to rise above and push through difficult times.*

2 Corinthians

Context- Paul needed to write to the Corinthians again. After writing the first letter, his message was well received, but his credibility was brought into question. When Paul addressed the issues they were facing, they did not doubt the message based on the teachings of Jesus. They did however bring into question Paul's authority in whether or not *he* was capable, or qualified, to teach these things. He was, and he said so. Paul truly suffered persecution for the cause of Christ, laying down his life time and again for the truth of his message. These experiences were his credentials.

For times of desperation

"For we were so utterly, unbearably crushed that we despaired of life itself. Indeed, we felt that we had received the sentence of death so that we would rely not on ourselves but on God who raises the dead. He who rescued us from so deadly a peril will continue to rescue us; on Him we have set our hope that He will rescue us again." *(2 Corinthians 1:8b-10a)*

Modern Application- There are times that you may feel as though your world is crashing down around you, and you may question why you were even put on this earth. God has rescued His people from desperate troubles before and He will rescue you. You can rest easy, because God is your protector. He is fully aware of your troubles and able to rescue.

Knowing you are not crushed, nor hopeless

"But we have this treasure in clay jars, so that it may be made clear that this extraordinary power belongs to God and does not come from us. We are afflicted in every way, but not crushed; perplexed, but not driven to despair; persecuted, but not forsaken; struck down, but not destroyed; always carrying in the body the death of Jesus, so that the life of Jesus may also be made visible in our bodies." *(2 Corinthians 4:7-10)*

Modern Application- Jesus changed the world. In dealing with stress, fear, and anxiety, those who follow Jesus have the God given power to deal with these struggles. Although you are not impervious to human struggles, you are never defeated. At a loss as what to think, you are never to give up hope. Ostracized and targeted, but never abandoned. Broken and beaten, but never obliterated. You can remind yourself of what Jesus did for you on the cross. In His resurrection, you have been given the power to live differently. You can be sustained in your times of trouble. With this there is no reason for fear even in the most difficult of situations.

For encouragement

"So we do not lose heart. Even though our outer nature is wasting away, our inner nature is being renewed day by day. For this slight momentary affliction is preparing us for an eternal weight of glory beyond all measure, because we look not at what can be seen but at what cannot be seen; for what can be seen is temporary, but what cannot be seen is eternal." *(2 Corinthians 4:16-18)*

Modern Application- The difficulties you face may drag you down mentally and emotionally. The struggles may seemingly have no end. The truth is that they will end. With your struggles God builds you up. The struggles that give you stress, make you fearful, and give you anxiety, are all tools God uses to make you stronger in Him. Your time on this earth and the struggles that come with it are temporary. Your troubles, although at the forefront of your mind and seemingly the most important thing in the moment, are miniscule in accepting God's love and forgiveness. Accepting Jesus and acknowledging that Jesus died for your sins, rose again, conquering sin for all mankind, gives you the ability to reunite with the Father for all eternity- where your troubles are no more.

For a troubled heart and mind

"So if anyone is in Christ, there is a new creation: everything old has passed away; see, everything has become new!" *(2 Corinthians 5:17)*

Modern Application- In accepting Jesus into your heart, you have the ability to be forgiven for your sins. You may feel the anxiety from the decisions made in your past. In accepting Jesus, you are recreated; your past is done. No matter your mistakes it is possible for you to be reborn in Christ.

Finding grace

"And God is able to make all grace abound to you, so that in all things at all times, having all that you need, you will abound in every good work." *(2 Corinthians 9:8)*

Modern Application- God provides all that you need through His grace. He provides everything that you need in order to live a life of good works—a life lived through, in, and for Him and His purposes. There is no room for anxiety and fear in such abundant living.

In times of weakness

"My grace is sufficient for you, for my power is made perfect in weakness." *(2 Corinthians 12:9a)*

Modern Application- God's grace can get you through any and all situations if you allow Him to take control and lead you where He wants you to go. It is in your times of weakness, when you are at our low points, that He demonstrates His powerful love for you. He guides you and makes you strong in Him.

Galatians

Context- Paul was prompted to write a letter to the church at Galatia after learning that after he had preached and taught there, the religious officials were adding to the message of Jesus, instilling their old-world customs and belief systems. This angered Paul greatly and he set out to remind the Galatians of the true message of Jesus.

Accepting forgiveness

"I have been crucified with Christ and I no longer live, but Christ lives in me. The life I live in the body, I live by faith in the Son of God, who loved me and gave himself for me." *(Galatians 2:20)*

Modern Application- People are quick to judge others. You are made in His image. Jesus died for all of us. Every sin for every person on earth was paid for by what Jesus did on the cross. If you can accept God's gift of forgiveness and His love, you are saved. The judgments of others are of no importance, because you are redeemed and are loved and accepted by God Himself.

In times of weariness

"Let us not become weary in doing good, for at the proper time we will reap a harvest if we do not give up." *(Galatians 6:9)*

Modern Application- In doing good and living according to God's word, you will eventually reap the benefit of doing so. In doing good things, you often feel as if your good deeds go unnoticed, are underappreciated, or even at times that you are taken advantage of, because of your perceived good nature. This can dishearten you and make you stressed. Do not become anxious by doing good; nor consumed or preoccupied with recognition and the approval of others. God knows what is in your heart; your motives and actions are noticed by Him. If you continue to do good according to God's word, and do not give up your resolve to do good, your actions will reap a harvest according to God's plan for you.

Philippians

Context- Paul wrote to the church of Philippi while he was being held under house arrest in Rome. Given the circumstances, one might expect Paul to be disheartened and less passionate in his writings. This was not the case. The letter communicates his passion for Jesus' message. He highlights the overflowing joy that becomes visible in those who follow Jesus' word.

In times of worry and fear

"Do not worry about anything, but in everything by prayer and supplication with thanksgiving let your requests be made known to God. And the peace of God, which surpasses all understanding, will guard your hearts and your minds in Christ Jesus.

Finally, beloved, whatever is true, whatever is honorable, whatever is pleasing, whatever is commendable, if there is any excellence and if there is anything worthy of praise, think about these things." *(Philippians 4:6-8)*

Modern Application- You have the ability to take stressful, fearful, and anxious thoughts and turn them into prayer. In doing so, what might be negative and crippling thoughts and emotions, become sources of hope. By praying earnestly and honestly about these things, God instills confidence in your heart and mind, bringing you an unequivocal sense of peace. The negativity melts away and the joy of God wells up, working through your thoughts, words, and actions.

Finding peace and strength

"I know what it is to be in need, and I know what it is to have plenty. I have learned the secret of being content in any and every situation . . . . I can do everything through him who gives me strength." *(Philippians 4: 12-13)*

Modern Application- There are times of happiness when you may feel you have everything you could possibly need in that place and at that time. It is the times when you feel as though you are lacking something that you feel stressed. God delivers you from these stressful thoughts. God's love and your security in Him is the greatest gift you could have asked for. You can be content in any and all situations. In times where you feel anxious or that you are not capable of acting, God gives you strength that you know could only be from Him.

Colossians

Context- Paul wrote to the church at Colosse. The people of Colosse were familiar with the teaching of Jesus, but were not in full appreciation of the magnitude of the life, death, and resurrection of Jesus Christ. Holding a mixture of pagan beliefs, holding Jesus on par with other spiritual figures and forces, the Colossians did not fully understand who Jesus was, and what He did for humanity.

Refocusing your thoughts

"Set your minds on things that are above, not on things that are on earth, for you have died, and your life is hidden with Christ in God. When Christ who is your life is revealed, then you also will be revealed with him in glory." *(Colossians 3:2-4)*

Modern Application- If you are able to turn your thoughts to the things of Christ, and the magnitude of what accepting Jesus into your life means. Your stress, fear, and anxiety of worldly struggles do not seem as significant and therefore should not paralyze your mind.

Accepting peace and submitting control to Christ

"Let the peace of Christ rule in your hearts."

(Colossians 3:15a)

Modern Application- Peace from stress, fear, and anxiety is possible with Jesus. Let Him take control of the things that trouble you; let Him rule.

2 Thessalonians

Context- Paul wrote a letter to the church at Thessalonica focusing on what is to come. A cornerstone in the teaching of Jesus Christ is belief in the promise that He will return.

Finding protection in your faith

"But the Lord is faithful, and he will strengthen and protect you from the evil one." *(2 Thessalonians 3:3)*

Modern Application- You may be confronted by those who claim to follow Jesus, or have your best interest at heart, but do not. It is up to you to believe and follow Jesus according to His word. God knows exactly where you are in your life. He will protect you from those who seek to destroy you; so that you can rest easy.

Finding peace

"Now may the Lord of peace himself give you peace at all times and in every way." *(2 Thessalonians 3:16)*

Modern Application- Jesus gives you peace from stress, fear, and anxieties in every way, shape, and form. It is up to you to acknowledge this, surrender the things that inhibit you. Give them to Him, and let God have the positive influence in your life that He promises.

2 Timothy

Context- Paul wrote letters to a young person by the name of Timothy in Ephesus. Timothy was a follower of Jesus, who Paul took under his wing in teaching how to spread the message of Jesus Christ. It is important to note that Paul did not work alone. He had a network of people spreading the message of Jesus. Timothy was one of these people. Paul focused his letters on the idea that human-leadership must come second to God-leadership; and people in leadership roles should follow God above all else.

Refocusing your energy

"For God did not give us a spirit of timidity, but a spirit of power, of love and of self-discipline." *(2 Timothy 1:7)*

Modern Application- *Stress, fear, and anxiety make you timid, second guessing yourself at every turn. God has gifted you with ability and talents that He wants you to utilize with confidence to better serve Him. If you can give your stresses to God, let Him relieve your burdens, remove the weight, then you are able to serve Him joyfully in the way you are best suited. With crippling fearful thoughts absent from your minds, you can function confidently and joyfully.*

For times you feel attacked

"The Lord will rescue me from every evil attack and will bring me safely to his heavenly kingdom. To him be glory for ever and ever." *(2 Timothy 4:18)*

*Modern Application- The judgments and rumors at your expense can often instill massive amounts of stress, fear, and anxiety within you. God is **fully** aware of these things and knows that the sense that you have no control has the potential to make you miserable. God promises that He will relieve your stresses from these situations; and that those who knowingly inflict these evil attacks will be dealt with accordingly in God's own time. You need not have any fear, because He is in **total control**.*

Hebrews

Context- The letter of Hebrews is written by an unknown author. The intended audience was Jewish Christians of the first century, but the letter is really for all Christians.

Sincerity in what troubles you

"For we do not have a high priest who is unable to sympathize with our weaknesses, but we have one who in every respect has been tested as we are, yet without sin. Let us therefore approach the throne of grace with boldness, so that we may receive mercy and find grace to help in time of need." *(Hebrews 4:15-16)*

Modern Application- In times where you suffer from stress, fear, and anxiety, you can rest assured that Jesus understands those feelings. He understands when no one else does. If you can be forthright, and honest about your thoughts and emotions, what the source of your troubles are, then you can have confidence that God will deliver you from what causes your troubles, because He loves you.

For when you feel abandoned, judged

"God is not unjust; he will not forget your work and the love you have shown him as you have helped his people and continue to help them." *(Hebrews 6:10)*

Modern Application- God does not forget the good in you. You may dwell on all the bad things you have done in your life and that may cause stress, fear, and anxiety. If you have accepted Jesus, your sins are forgiven, buried, done. With your sins forgiven, God enables you to do good. That moves to the forefront of your life and supplants your self-accusing anxious thoughts.

Feeling content in your current state

"Keep your lives free from the love of money, and be content with what you have; for he has said, 'I will never leave you or forsake you.' So we can say with confidence, 'The Lord is my helper; I will not be afraid. What can anyone do to me?'" *(Hebrews 13: 5-6)*

Modern Application- Pure motives and living to please God do not bring about feelings of fear. God has a plan for you. When you ground yourself in God, then you are never alone, never forsaken, and need never to feel afraid. God is your protector. No one is stronger.

James

Context- James was one of the early pastors of the church, and Jesus' brother. His letter was to all Christians.

In times of doubt

"If any of you is lacking in wisdom, ask God, who gives to all generously and ungrudgingly, and it will be given you. But ask in faith, never doubting, for the one who doubts is like a wave of the sea, driven and tossed by the wind." *(James 1:5-6)*

Modern Application- Every single one of your prayers is heard. Stress, fear, and anxiety are the products of doubt. When doubt enters your mind, you are cast into a whirlwind of negative possibilities. Often these mental formulations are worst case scenarios and you are thrust into panic mode. If you have faith in God and ask God for the wisdom you need to rise above, He will hear you and come to your aide. He frees you from these negative thought patterns. He loves you; He will provide the guidance you need.

1 Peter

Context- Peter was one of the most famous and charismatic disciples of Jesus. His letter was addressed to the followers of Jesus scattered throughout the Roman Empire.

Surrendering your anxieties

"Cast all your anxiety on him, because he cares for you. Discipline yourselves, keep alert. Like a roaring lion your adversary the devil prowls around, looking for someone to devour. Resist him, steadfast in your faith

. . . . And after you have suffered for a little while, the God of all grace, who has called you to his eternal glory in Christ, will himself restore, support, strengthen, and establish you." *(1 Peter 5: 7-10)*

Modern Application- Give your anxious thoughts and your panic to Jesus. He loves you and will not allow you to suffer a moment too long, if you seek His help. Satan may know your weaknesses, your fears, and what gives you anxiety. He wants to instill fear in you, and seeks to make you doubt Jesus.

Accepting Jesus into your heart, acknowledging what He did on the cross, and the triumph of His resurrection, allows you to overcome what was overwhelming stress, fear, and anxiety. Jesus is your protection. Let Jesus take away your stresses. Allow Him to restore, support, strengthen, and establish you, secure in Him.

1 John

Context- John was that disciple "whom Jesus loved." His letters teach us much about love for God and others.

Love for you

"There is no fear in love. But perfect love drives out fear, because fear has to do with punishment. The one who fears is not made perfect in love. We love because he first loved us." *(1 John 4: 18-19)*

Modern Application- Stress, fear, and anxiety are manufactured in your mind. Love, perfect love, is what God has for you to eliminate these negative tendencies you struggle with internally. You do not have to understand God's love for you in its entirety; but simply know that God has an everlasting love for you that reaches the ends of the universe. It eliminates fear. In acknowledging what Jesus did for you, asking for forgiveness and acknowledging the need for God in your life, you experience the love God has for you; and can love God in return. In being able to love God, you can then really love your neighbors as well as those you hold close to your heart.

Conquering your fear

"For everyone born of God overcomes the world. This is the victory that has overcome the world, even our faith. Who is it that overcomes the world? Only he who believes that Jesus is the Son of God." *(1 John 5:4-5)*

Modern Application- Those who accept Christ and are born again into God's kingdom have conquered all things. This means that you have no more need to fear, because your eternity is secure, beginning now!

About the Author

Andrew O'Donnell had made a successful career in financial services prior to transitioning to higher education. Andrew works in enrollment specializing in undergraduate and graduate academic needs assessments, along with enrollment and retention analytics in a university setting. He suffered from severe generalized anxiety disorder for over ten years. It is through his research and contents of this book that he was able to identify and overcome his anxiety. An undergraduate completing his Bachelor's degree from the University of Illinois majoring in Political Science with a minor in Classical Studies; he developed his ability to research both modern and classical writings and derive modern complex applications geared for today's audience. He graduated as an honorary member of the National Scholars Honor Society. Andrew then went on to receive the Provost's Scholarship while attending North Park University's School of Business and Nonprofit Management. He graduated from the Graduate School of Business with Master's Degree in Business Administration with a specialized focus in marketing. Upon completion, he was recognized as a Graduate of Distinction for superior academic performance throughout his Master's degree program.

Made in the USA
Lexington, KY
12 March 2013